SHOPPING
FOR GOOD

SHOPPING FOR GOOD

Dara O'Rourke

A Boston Review Book

THE MIT PRESS Cambridge, Mass. London, England

MIT Press books may be purchased at special quantity discounts
for business or sales promotional use. For information, please
email special_sales@mitpress.mit.edu or write to Special Sales
Department, The MIT Press, 55 Hayward Street, Cambridge, MA
02142.

This book was set in Adobe Garamond by *Boston Review*
and was printed on recycled paper and bound in the United States
of America.

Library of Congress Cataloging-in-Publication Data

O'Rourke, Dara.
Shopping for good / Dara O'Rourke.
    p.   cm. — (A Boston review book)
ISBN 978-0-262-01841-8 (hbk : alk. paper)
1. Consumption (Economics)—Moral and ethical aspects. 2.
Consumers' preferences—Moral and ethical aspects. 3. Consumer
behavior—Moral and ethical aspects. 4. Social responsibility of
business. I. Title.
HB835.O76   2012
178—dc23
                                                    2012024603

10 9 8 7 6 5 4 3 2 1

This book is dedicated to Cathy and Minju for inspiring me with their love and teaching me what matters most.

Thanks also to Niklas Lollo for research assistance, to Joshua Cohen and Deborah Chasman for their inspiring work at the Boston Review, to Jeanne Mansfield for editorial guidance, to MIT Press, and to each of the contributing authors for their lifelong commitment to working to move us from individual consumers to collective actors for good.

CONTENTS

I

Shopping for Good

On June 29, 2007, I waited in line for hours—something I hadn't done since college rock-concert days—for the privilege of purchasing a first-generation iPhone. From the increasingly frenzied media coverage, I knew everything about the phone's technical specifications: its processor, memory, screen size, camera resolution, software. But I knew virtually nothing of the story behind the phone. I didn't know where it was made, by whom, or with what effects on the environment, workers, communities, even my health.

My ignorance began to change as Greenpeace and other nongovernmental organizations (NGOs) launched campaigns highlighting Apple's use of toxic chemicals and the iPhone's contribution to the growing problem of "e-waste." By August 2009 reports started to surface in China about worker illnesses at a factory owned by Wintek, one of the contractors producing iPod and iPhone screens. In January 2010 Wintek employees went on strike over poor conditions, exposure to toxic chemicals, and resulting illnesses. Later that spring Chinese newspapers reported a spate of worker suicides at the Shenzhen factory of one of the main suppliers for iPhones, Foxconn.

Apple, revered as one of the world's most innovative consumer-products companies, almost overnight became a symbol of worker exploitation. Apple's core customers, usually unwavering in their loyalty, debated the scandals on blogs such as Apple Insider and Mac Rumors. After the Foxconn suicides, the technology critic Joel Johnson concluded in Wired:

> I can no longer look at the material world as a collection of objects but instead see interfaces, histories, and materials. . . . When 17 people take their lives,

I ask myself, did I in my desire hurt them? Even just a little? And of course the answer, inevitable and immeasurable as the fluttering silence of our sun, is yes.

Apple was forced to respond to these concerns. After years of ignoring their critics, a petition launched by a single Apple consumer on Change.org reached over 250,000 signatures. Tim Cook, Apple's CEO, then traveled to China to meet with Foxconn, something Steve Jobs never did. On the same day of Cook's visit on March 29, 2012 an independent audit of three Foxconn facilities was released by the Fair Labor Association (FLA) reporting that the factories were regularly exceeding legal limits on hours of work, not paying all of their workers for their full overtime, had poor systems for reporting accidents and injuries, and were running "unions" controlled by managers. Apple and Foxconn followed this first-ever effort in public auditing and transparency with public commitments to remediate workplace violations, including reducing working hours and raising wages.

In the past, scandals such as these would probably not have reached the public's attention. Few outside of the byzantine world of global supply chains had ever even heard of Foxconn, despite its position as the world's largest manufacturer of electronics. But today a global network of labor and environmental activists helps bring stories like Foxconn's to the mainstream. And as consumers become more aware of the labor and environmental issues behind their favorite brand and products, they seem to actually care more.

It is tempting to write off such avowed concern. Survey after survey shows that 30–70 percent of consumers say they want to buy greener, healthier, more socially responsible products. However, there is a massive gap between what consumers say they care about and what they actually buy. Yet it would be an error to disregard consumers as agents in creating more just and green manufacturing and supply chains. In the United States almost 70 percent of GDP is driven by what the government calls "personal consumption expenditures," a sizable portion of which is consumer products.

Not only do consumers have clout, but they potentially fill an important gap as traditional state and intergovernmental regulation fails to ensure ethical manufacturing. Global production systems continue to challenge the capacities of states, international organizations such as the United Nations, and NGOs to curb labor and environmental exploitation and human rights violations. Complex cross-border transactions, rapid movement between suppliers, and limited transparency have made it virtually impossible for national governments to regulate global production. The U.S. government does not regulate the production methods of U.S. firms operating in other countries (in part because of WTO rules), and the Chinese government has shown little inclination and even less capacity to regulate companies such as Foxconn, which is now China's largest private employer. NGOs, which are effective in advancing transparency and alerting consumers to problems in supply chains, are less able to monitor and enforce compliance with global standards and, aside from the threat of public exposure, lack mechanisms with which to incentivize supply-chain improvements.

Even in low-tech industries such as apparel, the supply chains linking the cotton fields of Uzbekistan, to weavers in Southeast Asia, to cut-and-sew operations in China have been more effectively influenced by consumer-focused campaigns than by national governments and international organizations. Consumers have directly targeted global brands, including Nike, Gap, and Levi's. Similarly, in electronics, consumer campaigns in the United States and Europe have done more to focus attention on resource conflicts in Africa (particularly those surrounding tungsten, tin, and tantalum coming from the Congo), water pollution, and labor rights in China than have government initiatives. Even when governments regulate—as the U.S. government has via new reporting requirements for conflict minerals—they often do so only after the launch of consumer-focused campaigns.

Consumers thus emerge as a crucial point of leverage: they can provide muscle for NGOs by generating feedback that can harm sales of global brands, pressure companies to change suppliers or to demand improvements, and they can create market opportunities for "better" products. Roberta Sassatelli paraphrases fellow sociologist Ulrich Beck, arguing:

> If modernity is a democracy oriented to producers, late modernity is a democracy oriented to consumers: a pragmatic and cosmopolitan democracy where the sleepy giant of the 'sovereign citizen-consumer' is becoming a counterweight to big transnational corporations.

Consumers, however, are mostly still sleeping and are rarely truly sovereign. We are often irrational and driven by habit, fear, and concern for status. But while consumers may not be the all-powerful citizens voting with their dollars that Beck and others hope for, we do have agency. And under certain conditions and given certain decisions, we can be reflective and sometimes even political.

The critical question is how big a role do consumers actually play, and can we do more?

What Is Ethical Consumption?

Calls for ethical consumption have existed since the early days of capitalism. The patriots who organized and participated in the original Tea Party boycotted British goods and encouraged coordinated consumer action. In the 1890s, the National Consumers League issued "white lists" to help consumers identify companies that treated their workers fairly. A continent away Gandhi's Swadeshi movement called for Indians to buy Indian-made rather than British products.

Ethical consumption today covers a wide range of issues and agendas. Fair trade and organics are the two most prominent areas of concern, but ethical consumers also care about sweat-free, locally made, union-made, and environmentally friendly products; artisan production; collaborative consumption—sharing instead of buying; slow food; farmers' markets; do-it-yourself manufacturing; non-genetically modified

(GMO) food; humane animal treatment; and voluntary simplicity.

Some of these approaches have rightly been criticized. Jo Littler, author of Radical Consumption, summarizes the critique against ethical consumption as a

> panacea for middle-class guilt . . . an individualistic form of politics, a means through which neoliberal governments encourage consumers to become 're-sponsibilised' amidst the atrophying of wider social safety nets.

But ethical consumption can also be an arena of political action and contestation, a place for politics to occur where they normally do not, or where traditional politics have failed.

Ethical consumption initiatives ask consumers to take a stand on issues such as global trade relations, poverty in developing countries, local economic self-sufficiency, environmental sustainability, workers' rights, and animal rights. Ethical consumption may mean buying different products—greener, healthier, more socially responsible—and it may mean lifestyle changes, such as consuming less, producing one's own goods, and sharing goods. These can be status-oriented, eco-chic consumer choices, or part of larger efforts to transform consumer cultures for the benefit of workers and the environment.

Health promotion is often a component within the broader rubric of ethical consumption, as personal health is connected to environmental issues and is an entry point for consumers into larger debates about consumption. NGOs increasingly focus on personal health as a means to achieve community and eventually planetary health. Organics are just one example. Many consumers think of organic certification as an indication that a product will be healthier because it does not contain synthetic pesticides and fertilizers. This may be true, but organic certification has more to do with farming practices, ecological impacts, and worker exposures than with consumer health.

A Booming Market

By almost any measure, the last five years have seen a staggering growth in ethical consumption.

U.S. sales of organic food and beverages rose from $12.6 billion in 2005 to $21.4 billion in 2009, growing more than 10 percent per year while conventional food and beverage sales were flat. Sales of ethical personal-care products grew from $5.3 billion in 2005 to $8.1 billion in 2009. In 1992 935,450 acres of U.S. farmland were planted with organics, rising to 4,815,959 acres in 2008. As of 2010 there were 6,132 farmers' markets operating in the United States; in 1994 there were only 1,755. In Europe sales of fair trade–certified products grew from 220 million in 2000 to 3.4 billion in 2010. Sales of local food, which travels less than 150 miles from source to table, rose from $4 billion in 2002 to $7 billion in 2011.

Overall sales of ethical products are expected to reach $57 billion by the end of 2011, sustainable apparel will hit $11 billion, and green cleaners $600 million. The U.S. market for LOHAS (Lifestyles of

Health and Sustainability) products is estimated at more than $200 billion.

Major corporations have watched this growth closely and jumped into the green, sustainable, and socially responsible space. Toyota Prius sales rose from 3,000 cars in 1997 to 28,000 in 2002 to more than 400,000 in 2010. Whole Foods sales grew from $90 million across ten stores in 1991 to $9 billion across 300 stores in 2010. Clorox Green Works went from zero to $100 million in sales in 2008 alone, Burt's Bees from $190 million in 2006 to $310 million in 2008, and Kashi cereal from $25 million in 2000 to $600 million in 2009.

New-product introductions are growing even faster than sales. In 2010 there were 72 percent more introductions of green packaged foods than in the previous year and 78 percent more introductions of green beverages.

Demand for ethical products is also spawning entirely new brands, such as Product (RED), and business models. The apparel industry has been shrinking in many developing countries since the end of the Multi-Fibre Arrangement in 2005, yet in just its first year of operation, 2010, one new sweatshop-free company went from zero sales to distribution at 350 universities.

Alta Gracia, which was built on years of organizing by the anti-sweatshop community, focuses on ethics and transparency. As John M. Kline describes it, Alta Gracia seeks to "help workers escape poverty rather than just avoid exploitation." All of the company's apparel—which is targeted at the collegiate logo market—is produced in a single factory in the Dominican Republic. The company pays its workers a living wage—more than three times the legal minimum—has encouraged the formation of a union, and meets the highest health and safety standards in the country. The factory is also regularly monitored by the Workers Rights Consortium, a leading labor rights organization. Alta Gracia interacts directly with consumers, who have a chance to monitor the company's work. For example, students in the United States can

Skype with workers in the factory, interview them live about their conditions, and learn about the effects of these jobs and wages on the community of Villa Altagracia. This takes Alta Gracia beyond even fair trade initiatives in connecting consumers and producers.

U.S. college students, their families, and collegiate athletics boosters are the key to Alta Gracia's model. These consumers have to care about, believe in, and act on their values by buying Alta Gracia T-shirts and sweatshirts, which cost more than comparable products, or the brand won't survive and thrive.

Creating Ethical Consumers

While sales numbers and brand growth are impressive, surveys indicate that there is significant room for growth in ethical consumption. Even the most popular ethically produced goods—such as organic milk and fair trade coffee—still only represent 1–5 percent of the total market.

Consumers report a much higher propensity to purchase healthy, green, and socially responsible products than sales show. When the Hartman Group, a survey research firm, asked U.S. consumers how often they base purchasing decisions on "concerns for issues such as the environment and social well-being," 76 percent indicated that they consider these issues at least "sometimes." In a survey by market researchers Mintel, 73 percent of respondents asserted that they are willing to pay a premium for green products, 44 percent said they consider the "greenness" of supermarkets, 31 percent of dry cleaners, and 29 percent of hotels and restaurants. In 2005 Datamonitor, another market research firm, found, "67 percent of consumers in the US and Europe claim to have boycotted a food, drinks, or personal care company's goods on ethical grounds."

With roughly two-thirds of consumers saying they care, why is ethical consumption so minimal and so rarely transformative?

David Vogel, a skeptic of ethical consumption, argues that beyond a narrow group within the population who really care and are already buying the products that match their values, consumers can't be counted on. In The Market For Virtue, he cites a study suggesting that consumers

> will only buy a greener product [if] it doesn't cost more, comes from a brand they know and trust, can be purchased at stores where they already shop, doesn't require a significant change in habits to use, and has the same level of quality, performance, and endurance as the less-green alternative.

This might indicate that the 75 percent of people who say they care are, to put it bluntly, lying. People don't want to admit to survey researchers that they don't care about climate change or workers' rights, so they exaggerate their concerns. But there are other reasons consumers do not act even when they have strong ethical beliefs.

A significant portion of consumption is more or less automatic; people just buy what they have always bought. Habits, routines, social cues, and heuristics are all critical to getting us through our busy and information-overloaded days. Consumers often accept the "default" option available in their local retailer, which usually isn't the most ethical.

Consumers are also influenced by sophisticated brand and retail marketing that induces non-ethical purchases. Through new tracking mechanisms such as browser fingerprinting, location-based identifiers, behavioral tracking, and supercookies (an advance on the common strategy whereby Web sites follow users' activities online by installing small files called cookies on their computers), online marketers use both consumers' real-time actions on Web pages and their detailed personal data to figure out which products they're most likely to buy. Retailers then put those products in front of them on their screens.

With loyalty programs, brick-and-mortar retailers, too, monitor what you buy, when you buy it, and how much you are willing to pay. These retailers are now experimenting with high-tech tracking and behavioral targeting in the aisles. A company called Video Mining helps grocery stores install systems that use more than a hundred ceiling-mounted video cameras to track and analyze customers' precise movements, how they navigate the store, what they pick up, whether displays attract them, how long they spend in each section, how a change in packaging influences them, and what they ultimately purchase.

Even when consumers can get past this direct manipulation, they rarely have the information they need to act on their ethical preferences. Consumers regularly report feeling simultaneously overwhelmed with too much information (a thousand shampoos to choose from), and limited by not having access to critical information (what hazardous chemicals might be in the shampoos).

Advancing more ethical consumption means taking on the constraints of habit, status, manipulative marketing, and information deficits. Progressive companies have a large role here. Just as retailers might manipulate consumers away from ethical purchases, progressive companies, along with NGOs, might promote them by marketing the value of ethical behavior.

One response to consumer habit is to offer default products that match peoples' interests and are better for the environment and workers. In a sense, retailers such as Whole Foods seek to offer this improved default and to convince consumers that everything in their stores is healthy and sustainable, although that isn't always the case. Companies are also increasingly selling ethical products by emphasizing the qualities that people already value in their purchases. Organic and local food have come to stand for healthfulness and better taste. The Toyota Prius offers reliability, energy (and cost) savings, and status. Patagonia jackets are well-made, stylish, and, again, high-status.

Using status concerns to promote ethical over conventional products works particularly well when people are shopping "in public"—that is, for products that other people can see, such as the Prius. These public products actually sell better when they cost more, a component of the status effect. Marketing and NGO educational campaigns use these dynamics when they feature a movie star such as Leonardo di

Caprio driving a Prius, helping to create desires that include ethical attributes.

The primary response to manipulation is to arm consumers with tools that help them affirm and act on their values in the marketplace. NGOs can take the lead here. The authors of The Myth of the Ethical Consumer find that "individuals who can recall the social features of their last purchase are more likely to utilize social features in their decision model." This suggests that consumers can be held accountable to their own stated values and preferences. Simply reminding consumers of their self-proclaimed commitments can be a powerful counterweight to conventional marketing messages.

NGOs have also been successful in combating the worst forms of manipulation and "greenwash," whereby claims of sustainability are used to market unsustainable products. Web sites regularly mock the most egregious assertions of global brands. The threat of a viral video or Twitter "bashtag" takedown has raised the cost of direct manipulation and greenwash.

Finally, social influence is also incredibly powerful in determining shopping decisions, and might be harnessed to positive effect. People are more likely to buy ethical products if others around them are. And this arrangement need not be limited to the physical environment of a farmers' market or Whole Foods: the lonelier confines of online shopping might also become an arena of beneficial social influence if social-networking tools can be brought into the online shopping experience.

NGOs and progressive companies should be involved in all of these methods of advancing ethical consumption: giving consumers information on the effects of their purchasing decisions, showing them that people like them care about these issues, offering ethical alternatives that match their values, and showing them the direct outcomes of their purchasing decisions, as Alta Gracia does with its Web-based links between individual consumers and factory workers. People are more likely to buy ethical products if they believe their choices have an impact.

A Way Forward

Serious work is required to scale up the most promising forms of ethical consumption and block greenwash. A number of initiatives—Alonovo, Skin Deep, Greenopia, ShopWell, Ethical Consumer, Project Label, Zumer, Climate Counts, Better World Shopper, Ethiscore, and BuyGreen, to name a few—have launched over the last several years to take on these challenges in different ways.

GoodGuide.com is just one example of these experiments, but one that I know intimately, as one of the co-founders.

GoodGuide began at U.C. Berkeley in 2005 as a research project aimed at understanding consumer decision-making. The goal was to go beyond surveys and focus groups to get a sense of what really matters to consumers—not what they say, but what they actually do while shopping. We gathered detailed data on what people searched for online and in stores, what issues they "filtered" for, and which products they ended up purchasing. In particular, we wanted to understand trade-offs in consumer preferences for health, environmental, and social attributes, versus preferences for price, quality, design, etc. In 2007 GoodGuide became a standalone social enterprise to help consumers see the full effects of the products they buy and the companies they buy from. With this information consumers can shop their values in the marketplace.

GoodGuide's staff of 20—including chemists, toxicologists, nutritionists, sociologists, lifecycle-assessment experts, computer scientists, and business and marketing experts—has rated more than 170,000 food, personal-care, and household-chemical products, as well as toys, appliances, automobiles, and electronic devices. The ratings combine product- and company-level evaluations to tell a consumer how transparent a company is about their operations and impacts, if there are hazardous chemicals in a product, whether it was tested on animals, whether the company has been fined by the EPA for pollution violations, whether the company donates more to Democrats or Republicans, etc.

All of this information—derived from more than a thousand data sources—is turned into a simple score from zero to ten (ten being the best), which consumers can personalize by using filters that reflect what matters most to them. One person can say they are opposed to animal testing and concerned about climate change, while another might say their primary concerns are labor rights and toxic chemicals, and these preferences are then used to determine whether a product passes or fails.

The rating is delivered at the moment a consumer is making a decision. GoodGuide provides iPhone and Android apps that allow consumers to scan barcodes with their cell phones and instantly receive product ratings while standing in a store. GoodGuide also developed a "Transparency Toolbar" that works within a Web browser to help people shop on Amazon.com, Drugstore.com, Walmart.com, etc. and see ratings filtered through their personal preferences right on those companies' Web sites.

The first lesson of GoodGuide has been that changing consumer behavior is hard. More than 15 million people have used GoodGuide.com and GoodGuide's mobile apps since they launched. However, this is still a small percentage of the consumers who say they want to shop with their values in mind. And even consumers who say they care are often busy, overwhelmed, and distracted. It has thus been a challenge to bring GoodGuide's tools to a large-scale user base.

From GoodGuide's users we've learned that information-based strategies work best when they are contextually relevant; the information is delivered at the moment of decision, easy to act on, credible, used by "people like you"; and the consumer is shown that a decision actually has an impact. GoodGuide's newest tool—the "Purchase Analyzer"—moves beyond providing product information at point of sale in order to stress this last factor: impact. The Analyzer shows people the effects of their past product choices and suggests steps to change their consumption habits over time.

We have also learned that personal-health issues are by far the most compelling for American consumers. Concerns about toxins in household products, contaminants in food, lead in toys, etc. increase with each scandal reported in the press. And, as mentioned, these personal-health concerns can be a first step toward thinking about broader community and ecological issues. Providing information about health effects is therefore critical to developing ethical consumption.

However, detailed scientific information, even on health issues, is not enough to change most consumers. Early on GoodGuide erred on the side of too much data and not enough advice. We learned that people sometimes want to dig into the detailed information, but they primarily want straightforward recommendations tailored to their preferences. In order to really have an impact, projects such as GoodGuide need to help consumers overcome entrenched habits by showing that there are realistic and affordable alternatives, and that making small changes has the potential to add up.

This challenge brings us back to the case of Apple, whose sales continue to set records amid the Foxconn scandals. This is partly due to the fact that consumers don't really have an alternative that is better. The entire electronics industry participates in the same supply chains, perpetuates the same problems, and often even uses the same suppliers. Amazon's Kindle, Microsoft's Xbox, and even HP and Dell's computers are made in Foxconn factories.

Despite any immediate impacts on their sales, however, Apple has responded. I believe this is due to the very real threat these exposes represent for their brand. As one commentator on the Change.org Apple petition explained, "As a Mac user for 17 years, this is the first issue that could make me stop buying from Apple." Labor and environmental issues may literally be the one thing that could hurt the high-flying company. Apple is thus taking action at least in part out of fear of consumers (and NGOs) connecting the Apple brand—which is now estimated to be worth over $150 billion—to sweatshops and toxics.

The question of course is whether Apple will move from reporting problems and protecting its brand, to actually solving the root causes driving these issues. One of the central lessons of the last decade of corporate responsibility work has been that monitoring and reporting problems in factories does not fix them. Apple needs to leapfrog other industries, and apply the company's core skills in design and systems innovation to solve the issues which are at the root of their labor and environmental problems. This will require the kind of revolution in manufacturing processes that Apple has brought to other industries over the years.

Critical in this will be for Apple to bring consumers into this process. From our work at GoodGuide it is clear that more and more consumers want to know about the environmental and social impacts of their products: where they're made, their environmental impacts, how workers were treated, etc. Apple will need to be more transparent with their customers about both the impacts of their production and their path towards improvements. Workers must also be empowered to participate meaningfully in addressing these issues, alongside labor, environmental, and women's groups.

Voting With Your Dollars

Many of the world's most pressing problems—climate change, biodiversity loss, industrial pollution, labor-rights violations, the obesity crisis—are driven at least in part by consumption practices. The bad news is that many of these problems are getting worse. The good news is that we are on the cusp of changes in the marketplace that may enable consumers to see better how their choices affect these problems and how changes in their consumption can make a difference.

Transparency is essential to changes in consumer behavior. This is an area where government policies could be playing a much bigger role. Governments can force companies to track supply chains and disclose ingredients and their origins, shining a light on the anatomy of global production. Governments also can regulate deceptive marketing and greenwash.

However, the goal should not just be for consumers to see production networks, but to have the opportunity to transform them: to send signals in the marketplace, to tell companies what they want in products, and to demand more sustainable and equitable systems of consumption and production.

A small percentage of consumers have already moved a portion of the market toward more ethical and sustainable practices. But the larger promise of ethical consumption remains unmet: to empower consumers to express their values—whatever they are—in the marketplace. If people could walk into a retailer or click on a shopping site and get instant information about which products best match their personal values, they could truly vote with their dollars. The big question is whether NGOs, governments, and progressive companies will work collectively to drive the market toward this more transparent and sustainable future.

II

Forum

Scott Nova

THE CONSUMER-ORIENTED STRATEGIES THAT Dara O'Rourke discusses are controversial in the anti-sweatshop and labor movements. Many activists and unionists are deeply skeptical of social labeling, product scorecards, and related approaches for several reasons:

• Under such schemes, multinational brands can win plaudits for small-scale and largely ersatz social initiatives and use the resulting goodwill to mask rampant, ongoing worker abuse in their supply chains.

• Vague, shifting, or non-existent standards, and minimal regulation, can allow companies to market as "socially responsible" products whose manufacture differs in no meaningful way from the sweatshop norm. Deceptive claims may become the rule, not the exception, in the ethical products market.

• Rating systems and scorecards grade on a curve rather than measuring companies against fixed standards. The resulting grade inflation can make corporations such as Walmart look like they are doing a decent job, and more sophisticated players, such as Adidas and Levi's, like heroes.

• Even if the development of a robust market for ethical goods leads to meaningful gains for some workers, the success may be oversold and weaken the impetus for deeper change.

These fears are grounded in experience. Over the last decade, activists have witnessed one empty "corporate social responsibility" initiative after another in the apparel sector, such as Walmart's "women's empowerment" program in Bangladesh, which provides training of dubious value to 2,500 workers, in a country where more than 300,000 people make

Walmart products for a minimum wage of $0.21 an hour. The program costs Walmart less than the value of the clothes Bangaldeshi workers produce for the company in half an hour.

The track record of apparel industry codes of conduct and monitoring systems has been particularly instructive. These programs, now utilized by virtually every major apparel brand and retailer, are the most fully articulated mechanisms to date for assessing and reporting labor practices in global supply chains. These regimes differ from the programs under discussion here—their purpose is not promotional but prophylactic: to protect brands from being publicly associated with sweatshop abuses. However, at their core, the two approaches are similar: both communicate claims about companies' labor practices as a marketing tool. The lessons are sobering. Brands and retailers have used codes of conduct and monitoring programs to convince key audiences that they have cleaned up their acts and are making a good-faith effort to protect workers in their supply chains. In the view of most unions and labor rights advocates, however, most have achieved this public relations success without any benefit to workers. Apparel-industry wages in many countries are lower in real terms than they were a decade ago; abusive conditions still abound; workers who speak out or try to exercise their right to unionize are fired no less frequently today than when these programs were first implemented. Factories where significant change has been achieved are the rare exception.

A more recent example: Fair Trade USA's effort to establish a fair trade apparel program in the U.S. market. Disregarding the vigorous objections of unions and labor rights advocates, FTUSA has adopted a wage standard that makes a living wage merely a goal: a factory can achieve fair trade certification despite paying workers the same sub-poverty wages as the sweatshop down the street.

Given this history, it's reasonable to expect a fully developed ethical products sector in which most companies attain the benefits of ethical marketing despite misleading, exaggerated, or downright false claims about labor (and other) practices. Even GoodGuide, a large improvement over past rating efforts and a useful tool for consumers, gives generous scores to major apparel brands whose primary achievement has been developing more sophisticated forms of empty rhetoric; it also rates companies that have adopted FTUSA's deficient apparel standard above Alta Gracia, the only brand in the field that actually pays workers a living wage (full disclosure: the Worker Rights Consortium helped develop Alta Gracia and wrote the labor standard).

I believe ethical consumption can be an effective means to advance workers' rights, but not without the following three components. First, high standards and clear definitions that enable people readily to distinguish the fake from the real, so that only companies that pay workers a living wage, treat them with respect, and are prepared to recognize independent unions benefit from a social label or a favorable rating. Second, recognition that social labeling efforts need to be part of broader activist campaigns; getting an ethical seal of approval will be a far more powerful motivator if combined with reputational pressure, and ongoing engagement by labor and its allies is the only way to keep any labeling system honest. Third, moving from ethical labeling as a form of special recognition to ethical labeling—and, more important, the labor practices necessary to earn it—as a minimum standard, one that comes as close as possible to replicating effective public regulation: forcing substandard products off the shelves.

Juliet B. Schor

I AM A GREAT FAN OF DARA O'ROURKE, WHOSE work on sweatshops and supply chains has been a tremendous contribution to both scholarship and activism. His research has improved our understanding of how to transform production systems. I agree with most of what he has written here, but I will concentrate on those areas where we may have some disagreements.

Like O'Rourke, I am enthusiastic about ethical consumption as an avenue for social change. In eras such as our own, when corporate power has increased dramatically and business capture of the state is so advanced, looking to consumers as agents of change may be almost inevitable. So-called "market campaigns," that work by pressuring retailers, have been some of the few success stories over the last fifteen to twenty years. But O'Rourke's account of how and why consumer activity can work at times veers toward what I would term the "naïve" model of ethical consumption, which assumes that consumers mostly have influence as individuals in the market and that shifts in buying power (or "voting with dollars") prompt corporations to respond. That is rare. O'Rourke does discuss NGOs, but I wonder if his account fails to give them enough credit, which is curious from a scholar whose work has been so oriented toward institutions, including NGOs.

As I suspect O'Rourke will agree, it is less by mobilizing people as consumers than as activists that market-based campaigns succeed. My research with Margaret Willis shows that the links between buying patterns and activism are strong. Using a national database of people who boycott and "buycott," as well as our own sample of 1,850 committed ethical consumers, we found that activism is highly correlated with ethical consumption and that 25 percent of our respondents were converted to activism through this route. In contrast to accounts that accuse ethical consumption of "individualizing responsibility," and therefore detracting from activism, our work finds that people buy and agitate as part of a single process.

This is also the lesson from a number of studies of particular campaigns. Activist groups play a crucial role in organizing consumers. Private, individualized shifts of purchasing power do not drive social change. Especially at a time when activism has been de-legitimated, ethical consumption is an important route into it. And without activism we do not get changes in state policies. Whether the issue is labor exploitation, energy standards, toxins, or animal cruelty, it is almost always state action that finally ushers in reform and takes change "to scale."

This brings me to my second point, concerning the strategy behind GoodGuide. Having participated in early, low-tech approaches of this sort, I appreciate their appeal. But as the field has progressed, I have grown less sanguine. In the literature on ethical consumption, a common refrain is that people are overwhelmed by information. They agonize about competing concerns, such as local versus organic, or fair trade versus low carbon. They feel paralyzed by multiple labeling schemes. While GoodGuide may allow consumers to set their preferences, the bigger problem is that they don't know how to weight them, not that they can't do the calculation once they figure that out. This model proceeds from an understanding of the consumer as rational and calculative. It's *homo economicus*, in the pre–behavioral economics era. But consumers are less utilitarian, more impulsive, and more symbolically driven than the rational model assumes. Enhanced information is a weak predictor of behavioral change. An information-rich phone is a gadget that feels like it was designed by an engineer for an engineer, rather than something that would appeal to a stressed out parent rushing through the aisles at the grocery store.

The alternative is to focus on companies and brands, rather than individual commodities. This is largely the way people already shop. Consumers can figure out which companies and brands best represent their values. NGOs can "discipline" those companies, as the food movement has attempted to do with Whole Foods. Learning that Patagonia, Ecover, and [fill in the blank] are industry leaders in eco-impact, for example, leads to a one-time, long-term decision. The convenience of a brand- or company-oriented approach should not be underestimated. Consumers are telling us they are overwhelmed by the task of choosing the "right" products, and they are begging for parsimonious solutions.

Social movements have always found the consumer goods that express their values. I am confident that today's activists can do the same, without expensive outlays on experts, rating systems, or hardware. The harder part is getting them to recognize that their individual purchasing power is less important than the power they can mobilize as an organized collective voice.

Lisa Ann Richey & Stefano Ponte

DARA O'ROURKE ASKS WHETHER CONSUMERS can transform global production. We answer, "yes," but not alone. While we agree with many of the points that O'Rourke raises, we challenge three.

First, consumers are not citizens without a state. Regulation and state intervention are still key factors in shaping the boundaries within which consumers make their "ethical" choices. For example, without subsidies and government mandates in the United States and the European Union, there would be less renewable energy for transport, perhaps none. Today, consumers can choose whether to fill up their car with straight gasoline or a 5–10 percent ethanol blend, or, they can buy an electric car. And recent changes in renewable energy regulation have encouraged the development of sustainable biofuels, made from forest and crop residues and even algae, not food stocks.

Second, while O'Rourke correctly observes that a large majority of consumers do not walk the walk, an increasing number do. In the early 2000s, critics dismissed the ethical coffee market as a small niche. As it grew they declared that it would hit a ceiling. And when the economic crisis hit, a dramatic slowdown was expected. Yet, consumption of fair trade, organic, and other sustainable coffee keeps growing—it's now more than 8 percent of the market. Another example: ten years ago, there were no wild-caught sustainable fish on supermarket shelves. Now thousands of products in more than 40 countries are certified by the Marine Stewardship Council (MSC), a nonprofit eco-labeling organization.

Third, O'Rourke suggests that initiatives such as Bono's Product RED are among "the most successful forms of ethical consumption." A portion of the profits from the sale of RED products is donated to the Global Fund to Fight HIV/AIDS, tuberculosis, and malaria. But there is an important distinction between "ethical consumption," which makes claims about a product (e.g., the conditions of production, environmental impact) and marketing campaigns that donate some profits to a cause. In our recent book, we explain how Product RED and similar initiatives are part of a new phenomenon we call "Brand Aid." Brand aid involves brands that provide aid, but also aid to brands. Brand aid helps to sell branded products and improve a brand's ethical profile and reputation. Brand aid does not ask companies to improve their conditions of production and thus is not ethical consumption in the sense that O'Rourke endorses.

Brand Aid, in fact, shifts attention away from the product—it doesn't matter how the products were produced, what the workers were paid, what the environmental impact was—to the cause, which, not coincidentally, has nothing to do with the product.

Fighting HIV/AIDS and tuberculosis is not only important work, but it also allows companies to do something socially useful without drawing attention to their production processes.

Labeling, such as MSC's, is critical to the future of ethical production and consumption. Ethical consumption relies on standardized practices that are guaranteed by labels. If the claims of supposedly ethical initiatives are not vetted then brand hype gets in the way, and consumers cannot make informed choices. O'Rourke's GoodGuide may help the rich and committed focus on truly ethical choices, but other consumers—poor, rushed, or distracted—will not be able to join the ranks of ethical consumers this way. Our solution is better policies that democratize ethical consumption.

Without regulation and state intervention to guarantee standards, Product RED and similar forms of brand aid are like greenwash initiatives that enable producers to raise their corporate social responsibility profile without substantially changing their business practices. All the while, consumers engage in low-cost heroism, unaware of how little difference they are making on behalf of people whom their purchases "save."

Scott E. Hartley

Dara O'Rourke highlights a dichotomy between what consumers claim to care about and how they act. I'd argue that there are two explanations for this dichotomy, one rooted in social psychology, the other in economics.

Regarding the former, people overestimate their positive qualities, a form of cognitive bias known as "illusory superiority." The norms that frame ethical consumption are aspirational, so it is reasonable to expect individuals to overestimate their ability to consume ethically. One might call it the Lake Wobegon effect, in which we are "all above average."

But economics is perhaps a more intractable obstacle to ethical consumption.

In 2007 I was invited to lecture at a national business plan competition in Tanzania, where I met some of East Africa's top entrepreneurs. The business plans I evaluated and the entrepreneurs I met fell into three categories. Some entrepreneurs were attempting to build an ethical consumer base; one explained to me his vision of bringing organic milk to East Africa. The second category was the "better-faster-smarter" plans for incremental improvement over the status quo. These can work, but they can be challenging to adopt unless the increased value is clear. The third category involved filling a void in the market. One entrepreneur who lacked any formal education explained to me that the backlog for baby chicken orders was months long. He sought capital to affix bright lights inside his vehicle to create a mobile egg hatchery. He would supply local buyers and provide a basic, missing service. His concept was business in its purest form.

In Tanzania I realized that there was a hierarchy of needs we often overlook in developed markets. Businesses address market gaps until they are filled and then create improvements until perceived value is outweighed by marginal cost. Only thereafter are consumers able to rationalize higher-priced products providing ancillary value. Ethical consumption is a luxury not all can afford. In Tanzania I nodded at the concept of organic milk, but one glance out my window revealed more pressing challenges. There were too many gaps to be filled, too many opportunities for improvement that would be addressed first. High demand for essential goods and upgrades in the developing world told me that, for a time, spades would trump hearts.

Ethical consumers, who are concerned about sustainable development, should worry about how Tanzania and other poor countries can grow despite fixed resources. Technology, insofar as it enables increased marginal return on the same input, can provide a necessary escape from the potential conflict between economic development and sustainability. True, the windfalls of innovation must be counterpoised against the externalities of production, such as pollution, but ethical consumers should agree that innovation and technology are the bedrocks of our ability to increase quality of life in a sustainable way.

Ethical consumption can foster positive, demand-driven change and to some extent influence the mechanics and processes of innovation. But civil society campaigns pushing ethical consumption must acknowledge that technology is the essential component of sustainable development. The realistic platform will embrace innovation. The ambitious platform will embrace innovation and pinpoint negative externalities, accepting that only when the initial pragmatics are met will we move away from our Lake Wobegon cognitive biases and toward action.

Government and civil society must work together to frame demand-driven change, with the needs of security balanced against the imperatives of human choice. Civil society will play a role in increasing transparency and access to information so that individuals continue to, with full agency, make the rational choices that match their needs. But the architects of change must weigh the goal of mitigating externalities against the benefits of innovation and frame the debate in a way that takes into account economics and psychology.

Margaret Levi

DARA O'ROURKE'S MAJOR POINT IS WORTH reiterating: consumers can influence which products are made, their quality, and the sustainability of both workers and the environment throughout the production process. I add to the mix the institutional consumer—universities, governments, churches, etc., especially in cooperation with key NGOs, labor unions, and sometimes a firm's corporate responsibility officers. But there are limits to any buying or boycott campaign.

If countries universally enforced the laws on their books, the result would be significant improvements in workers' lives. Yet this goal remains a pipe dream. Governments, contesting with each other for the business of brands and the location of factories, generally compete by offering lower costs. More often than not the state turns a blind eye to violations of labor and environmental standards. Too few countries attempt to win business by improving labor standards, management behavior, and consequent worker productivity.

Brands compete by lowering prices, usually through lowering input costs. Despite efforts by some brands to improve compliance with corporate codes through training and factory monitoring, the results are at best mixed. Compared to short-term contracting, long-term investment in local factories seems to lead to greater enforcement of national regulations as well as improvements in worker well being, as both growing statistical evidence and the Alta Gracia experience suggest.

To date, the most effective strategies appear to involve mobilization by organized labor or organized consumers. Changing consumer choices by making workers' rights an issue could precipitate transformations in corporate practice. Although ethical consumption campaigns have made significant headway in some products, such as specialty coffee and chocolate, fair trade remains a niche market.

That being said, institutional consumers can have greater influence on brand behavior than can private consumers. Indeed, many of the important ethical consumption campaigns are less about persuading the general public than ensuring that certain institutions change their buying practices. In the United States, United Students Against Sweatshops (USAS), possibly the most important instigator of effective ethical consumption campaigns, has achieved its greatest wins in university procurement. In almost every case, the Students have worked closely with the Worker Rights Consortium (WRC), which offers detailed reports of firm abuses, identifies the licensees who purchase from those firms, and provides a plan for rectification. The WRC, in turn, partners with in-country unions or workers' organizations.

At the University of Washington, where I am co-chair of the Licensing Advisory Committee, we participated in three successful campaigns to win benefits and terminal compensation long denied and legally owed to Russell Athletic and Nike workers in Honduras and to workers at the Guatemalan company Estofel. The demands of student groups, coupled with reliable information provided by the WRC and the Fair Labor Association, allowed us to threaten parent corporations with non-renewal of UW licenses. While the licensed collegiate apparel market represents less than 2 percent of their business, large sportswear companies fear reduction in brand loyalty and a loss of reputation. Universities can use the combination of their moral and scholarly authority to add credibility to the documentation of rights violations and do serious damage to brand status.

Without doubt, the economic well being of workers improves with the negotiated settlements of rights cases. However, in the vast majority of cases labor violations are not even reported, and in the few cases where grievances are filed, they usually fail. Sustainable improvements in the rights and material conditions of workers therefore depend on the enforcement by governments of national regulations and on corporate and factory self-regulation. Under-resourced and overstretched unions, NGOs, and activist groups bear an incredible burden as watchdogs, whistleblowers, and campaigners. So while the individual and institutional consumer are crucial for creating and sustaining ethical supply chains, equally important is a political strategy for making governments and corporations accountable for workers' rights and health. Success depends on a long and sustained campaign, as much political as economic. Only when states are committed and corporate cultures transformed can we proclaim victory.

Auret van Heerden

As consumers, we face hundreds of choices each day: what kind of shampoo should I use? Where should I buy a cup of coffee? What brand of shoe is best for my workout?

For most consumers, the choice is automatic; many will select the cheapest option, while others will make their decisions on the basis of habit or social cues. Each of these factors poses barriers to ethical consumption, and NGOs and campaigns have focused on asking consumers to change in order to overcome those barriers.

Of course, NGOs have created some innovative

tools to help consumers make ethical purchasing decisions more easily. These types of tools are essential, and many are Web-based so they can be consulted on smart phones. But there is still the problem of how to inform decision making at the point of sale. Activists have tried to guide shoppers by creating labels that should be instantly recognizable. Unfortunately, there is now a proliferation of labels, rankings, scorecards, guidelines, and phone apps that add further complication. And by asking consumers to consider so many ethical concerns—environmental health, resource conservation, ethical trade, workers' rights, human rights, animal rights—we risk making them feel guilty if one of their favorite products falls short. This atmosphere of anxiety and judgment may be part of the reason why only a small percentage of consumers act on their convictions.

If you play out each scenario for making an ethical choice, you quickly realize the difficulties. One option is to research online the products you intend to buy before you go to the store. Possible, but not very practical, and of no help when it comes to the "impulse buy." A little more likely is that you check labels to see if products have been certified by one of the initiatives that works on the issues that matter to you. Fair trade and organic products are easily identified, as are those that protect endangered species and certain scarce resources, such as ethically harvested woods. Those labels are generally reliable, especially when they deal with one issue, but the consumer can easily zone out when there are competing labels.

And what does the consumer do when there are no labels to guide them? This is where organizations such as GoodGuide come in, collecting data on products and categorizing it according to relevant criteria or filters. GoodGuide's smart phone app makes it practical to check on products even in the store, so there is no excuse for not making informed choices.

There is, however, a huge gap in the system of labels and guides when it comes to labor and human rights. Information about these issues is harder to collect and categorize. There are very few large-scale scientific surveys of the effects of supply chains on labor and human rights, making it hard for groups such as GoodGuide to rank the performance of different brands. Publically available information is usually concerned with specific cases or subjective reports and hence difficult to generalize. Information on labor and human rights is also likely to be qualitative rather than quantitative, making it harder to "crunch the numbers" for the consumer. Thus consumer-driven change in response to these rights issues is limited to individual cases. Reports of labor rights violations in the manufacture of toys in China led to only a short-term drop in sales of those products, although the reputational damage to the brand arguably lasted longer.

The only way to get brands to make a significant contribution to improving respect for labor and human rights in their supply chains is to get them to adopt a system of due diligence and remediation. The integrity of that system needs to be verified by independent external agencies. This does not mean that there will not be labor and human rights abuses in those supply chains, but it does mean that the brand has a program in place to identify and remedy them when they occur. That is as good as it gets and will enable to consumers to shop with greater confidence and thereby reward the companies that are really trying.

Rather than an all-or-nothing approach to ethical consumption, we should be more realistic: has company X made a public commitment to ethical production? Has it followed through on its promises in a timely fashion? Is follow-through verified by a credible third party? These are the types of questions consumers should ask. The smart companies will make it easy for consumers to find the answers, and those companies will set the bar for others in their industry who claim to be socially responsible. This could stimulate a "race to the top" which is supported, maybe even driven, by market reaction.

Andrew Szasz

SHOULD WE CHOOSE TO ACT ETHICALLY, mindfully, when the opportunity arises? Absolutely. Will such acts have societal and political impact? Perhaps. In the right context, under certain conditions.

If ethical consuming is to become a real force for environmental protection, two conditions must be met. First, ethical consuming has to become a mass phenomenon; the sum of many individual decisions sends a market signal strong enough to encourage manufacturers to change what they produce and/or how they produce it. Second, individual acts of ethical consuming need to be experienced by the consumer as only one facet of engagement with environmental issues, not as a substitute for—and possibly the end of—a more protracted engagement.

The first condition can be further broken down into three more specific components: the consumer must have trustworthy information; the ethical alternative must be competitive in terms of price and quality (effective, attractive, easy to use); and the ethical commodity must address issues that are important to large numbers of consumers.

Trust is undermined by pervasive false, or overstated, green claims—greenwashing. Dara O'Rourke's proposal thus has its greatest potential here: providing immediate, trustworthy information when purchasing decisions are made.

The need for ethical products to be competitive in terms of quality and utility has increasingly been met. Think of hybrid cars today compared to the first Honda Insight or the first Toyota Prius. Here the market has behaved as it is supposed to, improving products as it strives to give consumers what they want.

After that things get more problematic. Ethical goods typically cost more, sometimes far more, than their conventional counterparts. Consider, for example, of the price of organic meat, or the price of a hybrid compared with that of a conventional car. The premium on alternative products is a huge issue, a make-or-break issue, especially in down economic times. Income inequality in the United States has been rising for several decades. Median household income fell during the recent recession and has continued to fall in the "recovery." Officially unemployment is still above 9 percent, and 46 million Americans live below the poverty line.

Opinion polls show that Americans say they like a clean environment, in some very general, abstract sense, but when they are asked to rank the relative importance of issues, environmental preservation consistently comes in near or at the bottom, far below jobs, the economy, crime, terrorism, education, and drugs.

If the price gap and public opinion remain unchanged, ethical consuming will remain a niche phenomenon, restricted to a special group of Americans, no matter how good the information available on smart phones. Ethical consuming will continue to be a viable choice only for those who are already deeply committed and have the disposable income to afford it.

Ethical consuming could have substantial societal impact in one other way, though: if it motivated the consumer to become more engaged, more active politically. It seems obvious that if one is to choose the ethical alternative, if one is to shop consistently on the basis of ethical choices, one already has a nontrivial commitment to whatever cause the ethical product addresses: saving dolphins, say, or humane treatment of farm animals. But does buying the ethical product then deepen commitment and motivate further action? Or does it lead instead to a kind of self-satisfaction, a feeling that by buying ethically one has done well and that may be enough?

We know little about what one might call the *aftermath* of the ethical choice. Given how easy it is to shop, compared to how hard it is to take the time to participate in a movement, I would argue that ethical consuming is more likely to lead to a calming of concern, to a sense of "well, I at least have done something." Rather than inspiring additional action, ethical consumption is more likely to silence the internal voice that urges us on to do more.

If climate scientists are right, and I believe they are, we don't have much time. There is urgent need for a movement powerful enough to get markets and governments to act soon on environmental issues. Ethical consuming is a fine thing to advocate and a fine thing for each of us to do, but it is misleading to think that it will make a substantial contribution to the kind of mass activism that we will need if we, as a nation and as a global society, are to mount an effective campaign to tackle the crisis of our time.

Richard M. Locke

DARA O'ROURKE PRESENTS A STRONG CASE FOR
the role well-informed consumers can play in promot-
ing a more sustainable and just global economy. In an
economy shaped by global supply chains, O'Rourke
argues that nation-states, international organizations,
and even NGOs lack the capacity to adequately regulate labor, environmental, and human rights issues.
However, well-informed and well-intentioned consumers can fill this regulatory void by shaping corporate behavior through their collective purchasing
decisions. By "voting with their wallets"—either *paying more* for products that are greener, healthier, certi-

fied, and ethically sourced and/or *buying more* of these products rather than their less ethical or sustainable alternatives—consumers can drive changes in global business that will eventually lead to improvements in labor, environmental, and human rights practices up and down supply chains. Morevoer, O'Rourke's GoodGuide is a perfect example of how academic research focused on information and transparency can be translated into positive change in both consumer and corporate behavior.

However, the analysis provokes two questions that need addressing if we are serious about tapping consumers' expressed desire to improve global economic relations.

First, is shifting individual consumer purchasing decisions toward more ethical or sustainable or healthier products enough, or do we need to revisit underlying consumption patterns and the business practices that support them? Encouraging individual consumers to purchase better products is a step in the right direction, but it alone will not bring about the more systemic changes O'Rourke (and all of us) desire. This is because it doesn't address the underlying patterns of consumption in advanced economies that drive unhealthy and exploitative business practices. When it comes to products such as the iPhone, or just about any consumer electronics product, exploitative labor practices in suppliers' factories originate in our own consumer practices. The average life cycle for a consumer electronics product is about eight months. After that, consumers want, and are prompted to want, the new model: lighter, faster, with more memory and new features.

During that eight-month cycle, prices drop as often as every two months. This price erosion, along with short product life cycles, means that most retailers do not want to carry large inventories. So, they opt for more frequent shipments, often by air cargo, to meet volatile consumer demand. They thus avoid costly inventory while keeping shelves relatively well stocked, but in doing so they put enormous pressures on producers to deliver smaller, often customized, batches of products as quickly and cheaply as possible. In response, brands and even suppliers have developed practices that protect themselves—including pull-based ordering systems that signal that products should be assembled only after they are purchased at some retail outlet, just-in-time delivery of components needed to assemble the products quickly and flexibly, and "flexible" labor practices that enable factories quickly to hire and fire assembly workers in response to fluctuations in consumer demand/production orders—but these practices place a greater burden on the workers assembling the products. In other words, our desire for the latest model creates enormous volatility in consumer markets that can only be managed through a set of business practices that inevitably leads to excess working hours, low wages, and unhealthy working conditions for millions, who are often women migrant workers.

The relationship between upstream business practices and downstream (factory) labor conditions has been documented not only in the consumer electronics sector but in footwear, apparel, and elsewhere. Thus, if we truly want to redress poor working conditions within most global supply chains, we need first to address our own patterns of consumption—our desire for the latest products at the lowest price.

The second question provoked by O'Rourke's analysis is whether private politics, either through consumer purchasing decisions or transnational NGO campaigns, can effectively promote a more just and sustainable world without the active role of nation-states. I agree with O'Rourke that well-informed consumers, along with NGOs, can drive reputation-conscious brands and their suppliers to improve labor and environmental standards, but a decade of research on this topic by O'Rourke and others shows that these types of private interventions do not on their own lead to significant and sustained improvements. My own research suggests that private initiatives are most effective either when the state is already active or when private interventions complement rather than substitute for public regulation. This holds true for nations with relatively strong governments (such as Brazil) as well as nations whose governments are still developing (such as Cambodia). Likewise, many of the most innovative public efforts to promote labor and environmental standards—such as those in the Dominican Republic, Argentina, and Brazil—seem to rely on the support of private corporations and/or civil society groups for effective implementation and enforcement. Thus, rather than focusing only on well-informed and well-intentioned consumers, we need to explore more fully how private politics can enhance government programs to promote reform—and not one store or one factory at a time, but throughout the broader global economy.

III

Individuals Matter

Dara O'Rourke

DRAWING ON THEIR YEARS OF DEEP ENGAGEMENT with these issues, the respondents present very thoughtful comments on the role of consumers in influencing global markets. Despite a range of concerns, a consensus emerges among us that consumers can—and must—play some role in advancing more sustainable and equitable production.

However, the respondents raise important questions about how consumers fit within broader strategies and how acts of individual consumption can be scaled to make a difference and potentially lead to even more transformative collective action. The respondents also rightly point to the need to oppose the worst forms of greenwash and corporate-controlled marketing schemes dressed up as beneficial information.

In their specific critiques, the respondents point to familiar market manipulations, where consumers are provided suspect information, overloading or deceiving them (Schor, van Heerden); allowing companies to greenwash their images and get credit for token acts (Richey and Ponte, Nova); leading consumers to feel they have done their part and demotivating further collective action (Szasz); and undermining efforts to encourage governments to advance systematic regulations that achieve real improvements in global supply chains (Nova).

I agree that cynical versions of labeling systems, cause-based marketing, and "brand aid" should be exposed and resisted. And I don't underestimate the significant challenges to empowering and motivating consumers to act on their values.

But the fact that corporations have manipulated consumers in the past is no argument for ignoring or discounting the role consumers might play in the future. I believe we are at a turning point in efforts to advance transparency and enable new forms of consumer-citizen participation in the marketplace that respond explicitly to several of the problems identified here. Improvements in information technologies, supply chain tracking systems, environmental life-cycle assessment techniques, and behavioral psychology are laying the foundation for new systems of consumer information and engagement.

Despite these advances, there are good reasons to wonder about the role of consumers in broader strategies to advance sustainability, human rights, global health, and equitable development. Let me address three of these issues.

First, van Heerdan and Nova rightly note a lack of rigorous data on labor rights violations, and they fear that the softness of existing information may actually lead to worse forms of greenwash. I take this concern seriously, but I believe the answer is more and better information. Our capacity to monitor, measure, collect, and communicate information about global supply chains to the public is increasing. Having more stakeholders demanding this information makes it harder for firms to greenwash.

This claim is borne out by experience. When GoodGuide first launched ratings of household cleaning products, none of the mainstream brands would disclose the ingredients in their products. Due to a loophole in U.S. laws, household chemical manufacturers did not have to tell their customers whether there were hazardous chemicals in their products. A handful of green brands disclosed, but the mainstream, top-selling brands did not.

We rated these brands and "dinged" their scores for non-disclosure of product ingredients. Brands complained. But we made clear that we could not accurately evaluate the products without full ingredient disclosure. Faced with several NGO campaigns, a lawsuit in New York, the introductions of a number of state-level bills, and growing consumer demands to know what was in the products, all of the major cleaning products companies "voluntarily" disclosed their ingredients.

The process of creating public ratings, and of interacting with leading NGOs, academics, and firms around these ratings, has been critical to learning what matters most in each product category, what data is missing, and how we might collect it. By identifying this information, incentivizing leading firms to disclose, and pressuring the rest of the industry to catch up, we might be able to fill exactly the information gaps that van Heerdan and Nova decry.

Second, Nova and Szasz fear that ethical consumption initiatives demobilize citizens, undermining efforts to enlist them in political activism, corporate campaigns, social movements, and even voting to influence government policies.

Schor's research goes a long way toward addressing this concern. Schor finds that "activism is highly correlated with ethical consumption" and that "ethical consumption is an important route into [activism]." In other words, making even mundane product choices can be a critical entry point to deeper engagement with global labor and environmental issues and to further action.

Of course simply providing information on labor and environmental issues is not enough. Governments, academics, and NGOs have all provided too much data and not enough advice, "nudging," or empowerment for consumer actions. It is up to advocates, political organizers, and NGOs to provide the on-ramps to broader political action, and to show that these actions can make a difference.

Third, several reviewers suggest that any initiative focused on individual consumers—even if successful—cannot accomplish much.

I disagree. Individuals matter. Most technological innovations and social movements begin with small groups of early adopters. The challenge is always how to "cross the chasm" from this niche to the mainstream.

Even 5 percent of the market can be very influential. A small number of students have driven changes in the collegiate apparel market. Health-food customers drove early organics growth. Churches drove sales of fair trade coffee. As Margaret Levi points out, institutional purchasers—universities, governments, churches—are often central in this scaling stage. Scott Hartley may be right that not every consumer can afford the added costs of ethical consumption, but many who can still don't buy ethically. Support from governments and other institutions might help to foster their action.

One of the most successful movement strategies of the last 20 years has involved NGOs invoking consumers in campaigns to pressure reputation-sensitive brands and retailers to change. These NGOs not only wield the threat of lost sales from increasingly concerned consumers, but also present alternative, better practices (such Fair Trade, cleaner production, etc.), helping promote entirely new markets and then working to bring in governments to codify and regulate improved practices.

Finally, I agree with Richard Locke that we need to explore and build on strategies by which "private politics can encourage government programs to promote reform." Consumer-focused strategies should "complement rather than substitute" for government regulation. And in cases, all too common, where the government fails to act, consumer-citizen, bottom-up pressures can help to strengthen the backs of regulators. Ethical consumption does not crowd out government regulation. To the contrary, it has the potential to motivate it.

There is no doubt that we will need to mobilize individuals, along with advocacy organizations, institutional purchasers, government actors, and even leading corporations to address our most pressing environmental, labor, and health problems. The critical challenge is to design the tools, support systems, and policies that help to turn the everyday acts of millions of concerned individuals—as consumers and as citizens—into something that has the force to advance more sustainable and equitable economies.

ABOUT THE CONTRIBUTORS

Dara O'Rourke is Co-Founder and Chief Sustainability Officer of GoodGuide, an online resource for information on the health, environmental, and social impacts of consumer products. He is also Associate Professor of Environmental and Labor Policy at the University of California, Berkeley.

Scott E. Hartley is a venture capitalist and has worked at Google, Facebook, and the White House. He holds a BA from Stanford University and an MBA and MA in International Affairs from Columbia University.

Auret van Heerden is President and CEO of the Fair Labor Association. He is based in Geneva at the FLA's European office.

Margaret Levi is Professor of Political Science at the University of Washington and, jointly, Chair in Politics at the United States Studies Centre at the University of Sydney.

Richard M. Locke is the Class of 1922 Professor of Political Science and Management and Head of the MIT Political Science Department. He is a coauthor of *Working in America*.

Scott Nova is Executive Director of the Worker Rights Consortium (WRC) in Washington, D.C. Prior to joining the WRC, Nova was Executive Director of the Citizens Trade Campaign, a national coalition of environmental, religious, human rights, labor and other public interest groups. He is a graduate of Dartmouth College.

LISA ANN RICHEY & STEFANO PONTE coauthored *Brand Aid: Shopping Well to Save the World*. Richey is Professor of International Development Studies at Roskilde University in Denmark. Ponte is Senior Researcher at the Danish Institute for International Studies.

JULIET B. SCHOR is Professor of Sociology at Boston College. She is the author of many books including *Plenitude: The New Economics of True Wealth, Born to Buy: The Commercialized Child and the New Consumer Culture* and *Sustainable Planet: Solutions for the Twenty-first Century*.

ANDREW SZASZ is Professor of Sociology at the University of California, Santa Cruz and author of *Shopping Our Way to Safety: How We Changed from Protecting the Environment to Protecting Ourselves*.

BOSTON REVIEW BOOKS

Boston Review Books is an imprint of *Boston Review*, a bimonthly magazine of ideas. The book series, like the magazine, covers a lot of ground. But a few premises tie it all together: that democracy depends on public discussion; that sometimes understanding means going deep; that vast inequalities are unjust; and that human imagination breaks free from neat political categories. Visit bostonreview.net for more information.